# KEEP IT IN THE FAMILY:
## How to Pass Down Property Without Probate or Taxes

By

Laura Sanders, MBA

Creations PUBLISHING ©

*Spring, Texas*

*Keep It In The Family: How to Pass Down Property Without Probate or Taxes*
Laura Sanders, MBA
Creations Publishing, LLC
Published in Spring, Texas


For permission requests, contact:
Journey to Generational Wealth®
info@journeytogenerationalwealth.com
www.journeytogenerationalwealth.com
ISBN: 979-8-3495-2827-9
Printed in the United States of America

**Disclaimer:** This book is for educational and informational purposes only. It is not legal, tax, or financial advice. The author is a Financial Coach and Real Estate Educator, not a licensed attorney, CPA, or financial advisor. Readers should consult qualified professionals before making any estate planning, tax, or legal decisions.

**AI-Assisted Content Notice:** Portions of this book were developed with the assistance of generative AI tools to help organize and refine content, create planning templates, and format educational material. All content was guided, curated, and approved by the author. This work reflects the author's voice, expertise, and mission to empower families with actionable financial education.

# KEEP LEARNING, KEEP GROWING

## Explore More From Journey to Generational Wealth®

Your financial journey doesn't stop here. Continue building your knowledge, protecting your legacy, and positioning your family for generational success with these powerful resources. Each eBook is designed to educate and empower, and most come with a companion toolkit to help you take real action.

### The Smart Saver's Guide to High-Yield Savings Accounts (HYSA)

Learn how to grow your savings faster with high-yield accounts and make your money work harder for you.
**Get the Companion: Smart Saver's Toolkit**

### Money Market Accounts: What You Need To Know

Understand the differences between these account types so you can bank smarter, not harder.

### The Financial Foolery Detox

Detox from money myths, reset your mindset, and finally get clear on your financial goals.

### Keep It In The Family: Passing Down Property Without Probate

Learn how to grow your savings faster with high-yield accounts and make your money work harder for you.
**Get the Companion: Property Transfer Toolkit**

### Keep It In The Family: Why Life Insurance Is a Must for Building Black Wealth

Learn how to grow your savings faster with high-yield accounts and make your money work harder for you.
**Get the Companion: Life Insurance Readiness Toolkit**

### Legacy Matters: The Legacy Blueprint

A step-by-step guide to protecting what you've built and passing it on with purpose.
**Get the Companion: Legacy Planning Toolkit**

Shop all eBooks:
www.journeytogenerationalwealth.com/ebooks-toolkits

# DISCLAIMER

This content is for educational and informational purposes only and is not intended as legal, tax, or financial advice.

While I am a Financial Coach and Educator, I am not an attorney, CPA, or licensed tax advisor.

Before making any decisions related to estate planning, real estate transfers, or tax strategies, please consult with a qualified estate attorney, tax professional, or real estate expert in your jurisdiction.

Laws vary by state and individual circumstances. Use of this material does not create a client relationship or guarantee specific results.

Journey to Generational Wealth® is committed to empowering individuals through education; however, final decisions should always be made in consultation with licensed professionals.

 

# TABLE OF CONTENTS

# INTRODUCTION

Far too often, we hear of families losing the family home or land, property that parents, grandparents, and great-grandparents worked their whole lives to acquire. Whether due to a lack of planning, the probate process, unpaid taxes, or internal family disputes, what was meant to be a blessing becomes a burden.

This book is for families who want to change that, especially families of color who are determined to preserve the wealth and legacy tied to their real estate. Because that house or land isn't just an asset; it's a symbol of sacrifice, love, and generational progress. It holds the memories, sweat, and dreams of those who came before us.

Real estate is one of the most powerful tools for building generational wealth, but only when it is transferred with intention and protected with the right knowledge.

I created this book to guide you through the practical steps needed to maintain ownership of your family's property, avoid probate, reduce taxes, and ensure that your legacy is secure. Whether you're a homeowner, an heir, or someone preparing to pass down what you've built, this guide will help you protect what matters most.

Let's keep it in the family, where it belongs.

# YOUR TOOLKIT AWAITS!

Before you dive in, make sure you have the "Keep It In The Family" Property Transfer Toolkit by your side. This companion resource includes **fillable worksheets, checklists, and planning templates** to help you **take action** and **protect your legacy with clarity and confidence.**

You're not just here to learn - you're here to build.

**Visit:** www.journeytogenerationalwealth.com/product-page/propertytransfertoolkit

# CHAPTER 1: UNDERSTANDING THE THREATS

Before we dive into how to pass down property and land the right way, it's important to first understand the problems that can arise when families don't have a plan. These issues can not only delay inheritance but also create family drama, legal disputes, and unnecessary tax burdens. Let's look at the biggest threats to your family's legacy.

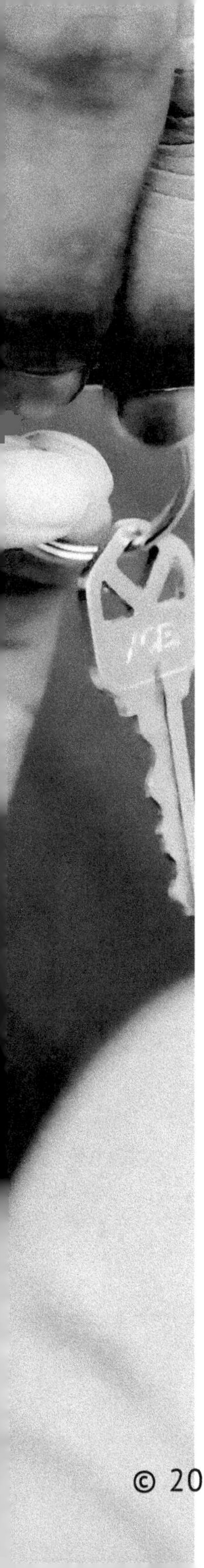

# WHAT IS PROBATE AND WHY YOU WANT TO AVOID IT

**Probate** is the legal process by which the court distributes a deceased person's assets. If a property owner dies without a proper estate plan, their real estate will likely go through probate, even if they have a will.

**Problems with Probate:**

- **Time-Consuming:** Probate can take 6 months to 2 years to finalize.
- **Expensive:** Court fees, attorney fees, and executor fees can eat up 5%–10% (or more) of the estate's value.
- **Public:** All probate records are public, meaning anyone can see what your family owned and who got what.
- **Risk of Disputes:** Probate opens the door to legal challenges from estranged family members or creditors.

**Bottom Line:** *If you want your heirs to receive property quickly, privately, and without court interference, you must avoid probate.*

# WHEN AND WHY INHERITANCE TAXES APPLY

Inheritance taxes and estate taxes are often misunderstood, but they are very real for families who don't plan ahead.

**Key Terms:**
**Estate Tax:** A federal (and sometimes state) tax on the value of the estate before it's passed on.
**Inheritance Tax:** A state-level tax some heirs may owe on what they receive.

**Current Federal Estate Tax (2025):**
Exemption: $13.61 million per person
Married couples: $27.22 million with proper planning

*Expected Federal Estate Tax (2026):*
Exemption: $15 million per person
Married couples: $30 million with proper planning

Most families won't owe federal estate taxes, but if property appreciates or if your state has its own inheritance or estate tax, your family could be hit.

**Action Tip:** Know your state's rules. States like Maryland, New Jersey, and Nebraska do have inheritance or estate taxes.

 

# COMMON MISTAKES THAT CAUSE PROPERTY LOSS

Many families lose property simply because they never took the time to prepare. Here are some of the most common mistakes:

- **No will or trust in place**
- **Only one person listed on the deed**
- **Failure to update deeds after death**
- **Assuming a will alone avoids probate (it doesn't!)**
- **Co-ownership with someone who later divorces or files bankruptcy**
- **Not paying property taxes**

**Real Talk:** Title issues and probate delays can force heirs to sell the property just to pay court fees or taxes. These mistakes are avoidable with planning.

# WHAT HAPPENS WHEN A DEED HAS ONLY ONE NAME

If the property deed is only in one person's name and that person passes away:

- The property is considered part of their estate.
- It will go through probate unless a trust or TOD (Transfer on Death) deed is in place.
- If the deceased didn't have a will, the court uses state laws to decide who inherits, which may not reflect their actual wishes.

**Example:**
Grandma leaves behind the family house. Her name is the only one on the deed. She never created a will or trust. Now, you and your siblings must go to probate court and spend months, and thousands of dollars, before you can legally own or sell the house.

**Bottom Line:** This can be avoided by setting up proper ownership and beneficiary plans while you're still alive.

 

# THE BIG TAKEAWAY

If you own land or property and want to protect it from the government, legal fees, and potential family disputes, you need to act now. Failing to plan doesn't just affect you; it can divide your family, destroy generational wealth, and cost your heirs time and money.

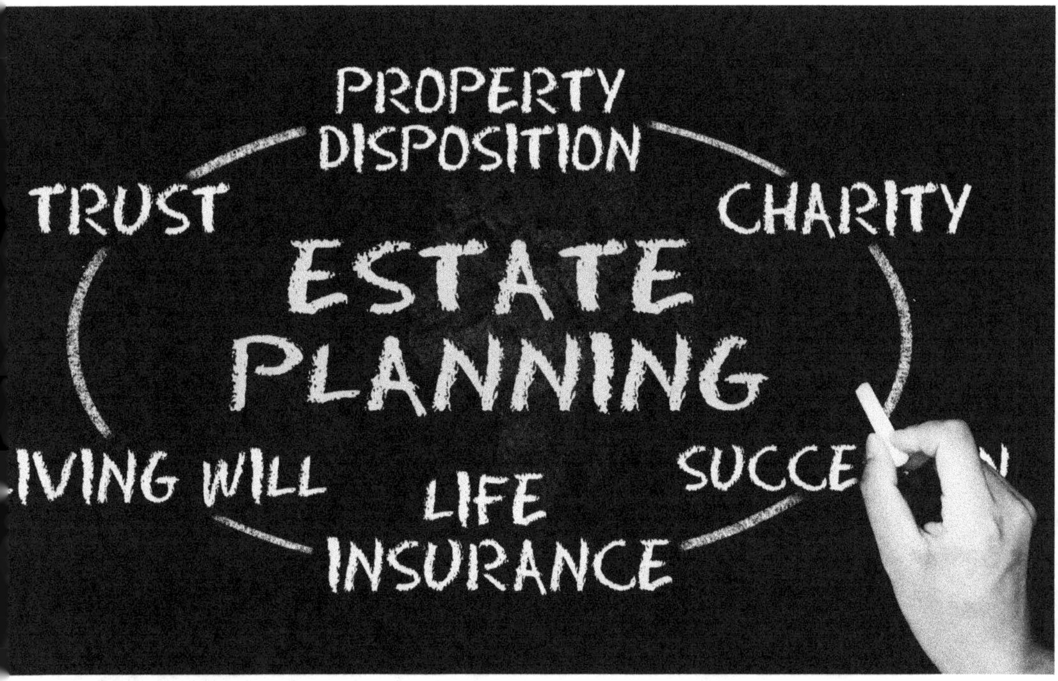


 

# CHAPTER 2: HOW TO PROTECT YOUR PROPERTY AND AVOID PROBATE

If you want your family to inherit land or property without delay, drama, or court involvement, take legal action now, not later. The good news? There are proven, legally sound strategies to transfer property that avoid probate entirely. In this chapter, you'll learn how to protect your assets with simple, effective tools that can secure your legacy for generations to come.

# CREATE A REVOCABLE LIVING TRUST

A **Revocable Living Trust** is one of the most powerful and flexible tools for passing down property outside of probate.

**How It Works:**

- You create a trust and transfer the title of your property into it.
- You are the trustee and beneficiary while you're alive, so you keep control.
- Upon your death, the **successor trustee** you named transfers the property to your heirs **without probate**.

**Key Benefits:**

- Avoids probate
- Keeps your affairs private
- Maintains control during your lifetime
- Can include multiple properties or assets

Recommended for families with multiple heirs or significant assets.

# USE A TRANSFER ON DEATH (TOD) DEED OR BENEFICIARY DEED

Depending on your state, you may be able to file a **Transfer on Death Deed**, also called a **Beneficiary Deed**.

**How it Works:**

- You record the deed while you're alive and name a beneficiary.
- You retain full control, ownership, and the ability to sell or refinance the property.
- When you pass away, the property automatically transfers to the named person, no probate required.

**Pros:**

- Simple, inexpensive, and avoids probate
- Allows you to maintain full control during your lifetime
- Reversible: You can change or revoke the TOD deed at any time
- Does not trigger gift tax at the time of recording

**Cons:**

- **Not Available in All States:** Not every state allows TOD deeds. You must confirm your state's laws.
- **Potential for Errors:** Mistakes in how the deed is prepared or filed (e.g., not recording it properly) can invalidate it and force the property through probate anyway.
- **Limited to Real Property:** TOD deeds apply only to real estate, not bank accounts, vehicles, or other assets.
- **No Asset Protection:** If your named beneficiary has debts or legal judgments, creditors may be able to claim the property after your death.
- **No Contingency Planning:** If your beneficiary dies before you (and you don't update the deed), the property may still end up in probate.

**Note:** TOD deeds are a great low-cost option for simple estate plans, but they still require careful execution and should be reviewed periodically to ensure they reflect your current wishes.

 

# CONSIDER A LIFE ESTATE DEED

A **Life Estate Deed** allows you to retain ownership and use of your home during your lifetime, while naming someone else to automatically receive it upon your death.

**Example:**
You name your daughter as the "remainderman." You live in the house for the rest of your life, and she automatically inherits it when you pass, with no need for probate.

**Important Considerations:**

- Avoids probate
- You can't sell or refinance without the remainderman's permission
- May impact Medicaid eligibility

**Bottom Line:** Best used when you're confident you won't need to sell or mortgage the property.

# USE JOINT OWNERSHIP WITH RIGHT OF SURVIVORSHIP (JTWROS)

Adding another person to your deed with **right of survivorship** means they automatically inherit the property when you pass.

**Types:**

- **Joint Tenancy with Right of Survivorship**
- **Tenancy by the Entirety** (for married couples)

**Pros:**

- Simple and automatic transfer upon death
- Avoids probate

**Cons:**

- Immediate loss of full control
- May trigger gift taxes
- Exposes the property to the co-owner's creditors, divorce, or legal issues

Not ideal unless you fully trust the co-owner and understand the risks.

# COMBINE TOOLS FOR BETTER PROTECTION

Many families use a combination of tools, such as:

- A living trust for flexibility and privacy
- TOD deeds for individual properties
- Wills to cover assets not included in the trust

Proper estate planning is not one-size-fits-all. The right strategy depends on your family's goals, the value of the property, and your state's laws.

# SUMMARY: WHAT YOU SHOULD CONSIDER NOW

| Strategy | Probate-Free | Keeps Control | Private | Notes |
|---|---|---|---|---|
| Living Trust | ✓ | ✓ | ✓ | Best all-around protection |
| TOD/Beneficiary Deed | ✓ | ✓ | X | State-specific availability |
| Life Estate Deed | ✓ | X | X | Risk of reduced flexibility |
| Joint Ownership (JTWROS) | ✓ | X | X | Potential legal and financial risks |

# ACTION STEP:

Talk to a qualified estate planning attorney in your state to:

- Set up a revocable living trust
- File the appropriate deed (TOD, life estate, or joint ownership)
- Draft a will that complements your deed or trust
- Ensure your documents align with your long-term legacy goals

**Tip:** Be sure to source multiple estate attorneys to ensure the one you choose to work with is the best fit for you and your budget.

Seriously, I found out after it was to late that I overpaid for my estate plan. Talk about upset, I don't even want to talk about it.

# CHAPTER 3: HOW TO MINIMIZE OR AVOID INHERITANCE TAXES

Inheritance taxes may not affect every family, but when they do, the cost can be devastating. Even if your estate falls below the federal threshold, property passed down without a plan can trigger **capital gains taxes, state-level estate taxes,** or **loss of wealth** that could have been prevented.

In this chapter, we'll walk through the best strategies to keep more of your property's value in your family's hands, and out of the hands of the IRS or your state government.

# 1. UNDERSTAND WHAT TAXES YOU'RE ACTUALLY FACING

There are three key types of taxes to be aware of when transferring property:

**1. Federal Estate Tax**
This is a tax on the total value of a deceased person's estate before it's passed to heirs.
**Updated 2025 Federal Exemption:**
As of July 4, 2025, the federal estate and gift tax exemption has been **permanently** increased to:

- **$15 million per person**
- **$30 million for married couples** (with portability)

This means only estates exceeding these thresholds will owe federal estate tax. For most families, this new limit removes the concern of paying federal estate tax—though proper planning is still essential to avoid probate, reduce capital gains, and address state-level taxes.

**2. State Estate or Inheritance Tax**
While most estates won't owe federal estate tax under the new exemption, several states **still impose their own estate or inheritance taxes,** often with **much lower thresholds** (as low as $1 million).

- States like **Maryland, Oregon, Minnesota**, and **New York** impose their own **estate taxes**.
- States like **Iowa, Kentucky, Nebraska**, and **Pennsylvania** impose an inheritance tax on the person receiving the property, not the estate itself.

**Action Step:** Research your state's laws to determine if your family could owe taxes even if you fall under the federal exemption.

 

**3. Capital Gains Tax**

- If your heir sells the inherited property and it has appreciated, they may owe capital gains tax on the increase in value.
- This is often where families lose money unnecessarily, especially if the property is gifted too soon.

# 2. TAKE ADVANTAGE OF THE STEP-UP IN BASIS

The **Step-Up in Basis** is one of the most valuable tax benefits in estate planning.

**Here's how it works:**

- If your property appreciated during your lifetime, your heirs **do not inherit your original purchase price**.
- Instead, they receive the property **with a new tax basis equal to its value at the date of your death.**
- This means if they sell the property right away, they pay little to no capital gains tax.

**Example:**
You bought land for $100,000. It's worth $350,000 when you pass.

- Without step-up: Heirs pay tax on $250,000 gain.
- With step-up: The basis is now $350,000. If they sell for $360,000, they only owe tax on $10,000.

**Warning:** If you give property away while living (instead of leaving it in a will or trust), your heir gets your original basis and loses the step-up benefit.

# 3. AVOID GIFTING THE PROPERTY DURING YOUR LIFETIME (UNLESS STRATEGICALLY PLANNED)

Many people think, "I'll just sign the deed over now." But giving property as a living gift can backfire.

**Risks of Lifetime Gifting:**

- **No step-up in basis** = higher capital gains tax
- May trigger **gift tax reporting** if the property is worth more than the annual exclusion ($19,000 in 2025)
- Loss of control and potential issues with Medicaid eligibility

Only gift during your lifetime if advised by a tax or estate planning professional, and only as part of a bigger strategy.

 

# 4. USE A TRUST TO AVOID PROBATE AND PRESERVE TAX BENEFITS

When you place property into a **revocable living trust**, your heirs:

- Avoid probate
- Still qualify for the step-up in basis
- Gain immediate access to the property without delay

Optional: Use an **Irrevocable Trust** if you:

- Want to reduce your estate size
- Are you planning for Medicaid
- Want strong protection from lawsuits or creditors

Trusts offer both **privacy** and **tax efficiency**, a winning combination.

# 5. USE THE ANNUAL GIFT EXCLUSION AND LIFETIME EXEMPTION (ADVANCED STRATEGY)

If you expect your estate to exceed the federal limit, you can reduce its size while you're alive using tax-free gifting.

**Gift Tax Basics (2025 limits):**

- **Annual exclusion:** $19,000 per recipient per year
- **Lifetime exemption:** $13.99 million (matches the estate tax threshold)

**Example:**

- You and your spouse can gift $38,000 per child per year.
- This removes assets from your taxable estate while helping your family now.

**Important:** Gifting property still loses the step-up in basis, so this strategy is best for non-appreciated assets or cash.

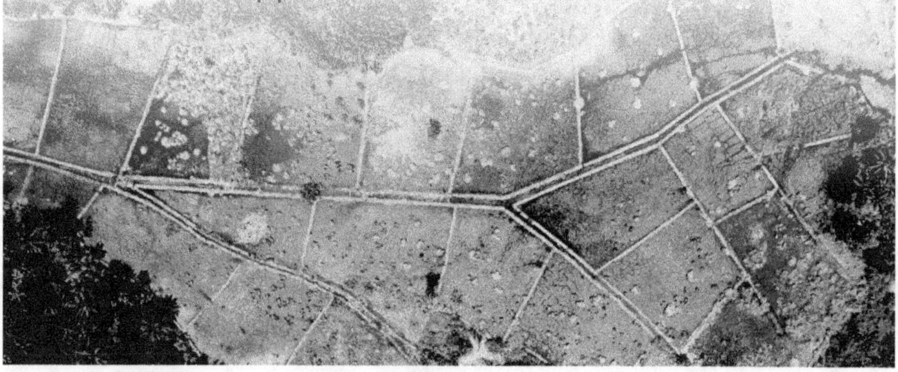

# 6. PLAN NOW, BEFORE THE LAW CHANGES

Under current law, the estate tax exemption is set to be **cut in half** at the end of 2025, reverting to around **$6–7 million per person** unless new legislation is passed.

This means:

- More families may be exposed to estate taxes starting in 2026.
- Planning ahead now ensures your property is protected under today's rules.

**Quick Action Checklist**

- ☐ Confirm your estate's value and whether it could be taxed
- ☐ Know your state's inheritance and estate tax rules
- ☐ Avoid gifting appreciated property during your lifetime
- ☐ Use a trust to pass property and preserve step-up in basis
- ☐ Consider using the gift exclusion for wealth you don't want to appreciate
- ☐ Talk with a tax advisor before transferring any real estate

**Final Word:**

Smart tax planning can make the difference between building a family legacy, or watching wealth disappear through unnecessary taxes, and delays. **The earlier you plan, the more you preserve.**

 

# CHAPTER 4: ACTION PLAN FOR FAMILIES

**Secure the Legacy. Protect Your Property. Empower the Next Generation.**

Now that you understand the threats (Chapter 1), the tools to avoid probate (Chapter 2), and how to minimize taxes (Chapter 3), it's time to put that knowledge into action.

This chapter lays out a step-by-step plan to help you and your family protect your property, avoid court and tax traps, and ensure your heirs are set up to receive it smoothly and securely.

# STEP 1. MEET WITH AN ESTATE PLANNING ATTORNEY

This is your first and most crucial step. A qualified attorney will:

- Review your assets and family situation
- Help you choose the best tools for your goals (e.g., trust, TOD deed, will)
- Ensure your documents comply with your state's laws
- Record any necessary deeds or changes in title

**Pro Tip:** Choose an attorney who specializes in both estate planning and real estate law. Bring a copy of your current deed to the meeting.

# STEP 2. DETERMINE THE BEST STRATEGY FOR YOUR STATE

Each state has different rules about:

- **Transfer on Death (TOD) Deeds**
- **Inheritance and estate taxes**
- **Probate court processes**
- **Community property vs. common law property**

**Your Options May Include:**

| Tool | States That Allow It | Purpose |
|---|---|---|
| **TOD Deed** | ~30+ states | Avoids probate for real estate |
| **Life Estate Deed** | Most states | Simplified probate avoidance |
| **Revocable Living Trust** | All states | Comprehensive estate plan |

Check with your attorney or local Recorder of Deeds office to confirm what's legal in your state.

 

# STEP 3. ESTABLISH A REVOCABLE LIVING TRUST (STRONGLY RECOMMENDED)

Even if you live in a state that allows TOD deeds, a **living trust** offers greater flexibility and privacy, especially if:

- You own multiple properties
- You have minor or financially inexperienced heirs
- You want to control how and when heirs receive assets

**Key Actions:**

- Create the trust and name yourself as trustee
- Name a successor trustee and your beneficiaries
- Retitle the property into the name of the trust
- Update your homeowner's insurance to reflect the trust name

 

# STEP 4. KEEP PROPERTY-RELATED RESPONSIBILITIES UP-TO-DATE

Even the best estate plan can fail if the property is lost due to unpaid taxes or lack of maintenance.

Make sure to:

- Stay current on **property taxes and insurance**
- Maintain the home to prevent depreciation or loss
- Avoid liens (e.g., unpaid bills, HOA fees, judgments)

**Bonus Tip:** Keep a copy of the deed, title, and estate plan in a fireproof safe and provide access instructions to your successor trustee or executor.

 

# STEP 5. COMMUNICATE WITH YOUR HEIRS NOW

A plan is only powerful if your heirs know about it.

**What to Share:**

- What property or land they will inherit
- What legal tools you've used (trust, deed, etc.)
- Who will manage the transition (successor trustee or executor)
- Where documents are stored

**Consider holding a family meeting** with your attorney or financial advisor present to ensure clarity and prevent future conflict.

# STEP 6: ADD PROTECTION PROVISIONS

Consider these advanced but critical options:

- **Bloodline Trusts** to protect property from in-laws and divorce
- **Spendthrift Clauses** to prevent irresponsible use
- **LLC or Family Trust Ownership** for shared properties (e.g., farmland, rental properties, legacy homes)

These additions can:

- Keep property in the family line
- Prevent court battles between heirs
- Add legal and financial protection for generations

 

# STEP 7: UPDATE YOUR PLAN AS LIFE CHANGES

Review your plan every 2–3 years or whenever there's a major change in:

- Marital status
- Family structure (birth, death, divorce)
- Property ownership
- Financial or health status
- Laws impacting estate and tax planning

Don't set it and forget it. A great estate plan is a living document.

# FAMILY LEGACY PLANNING WORKSHEET

Track key legacy planning actions to ensure your family's property and wishes are protected.

| Action Item | Completed (✓) | Notes |
|---|---|---|
| Met with attorney | | |
| Reviewed deed(s) | | |
| Created a trust or TOD deed | | |
| Retitled property correctly | | |
| Stored documents securely | | |
| Communicated with heirs | | |
| Added protective clauses | | |
| Scheduled plan review | | |

**Final Thought:**

**Don't just leave behind a house, leave behind a plan.** Your family's wealth, peace, and future depend on it.

 

# CHAPTER 5: PROTECTING HEIRS FROM FUTURE TAX ISSUES

**You've Passed Down the Property. Now Help Them Keep It.**

You've done the hard work, planned your estate, avoided probate, and transferred property to your loved ones. But the journey doesn't stop there.

**The next challenge?** Making sure your heirs don't lose the very inheritance you worked so hard to protect.

Without proper education and planning, heirs can unknowingly trigger taxes, fall behind on obligations, or even be forced to sell. This chapter shows how to equip your heirs with the knowledge, tools, and strategies to preserve their inheritance for the long term.

 

# 1. EDUCATE HEIRS ON PROPERTY OWNERSHIP RESPONSIBILITIES

When someone inherits property, they often aren't prepared for what comes next, especially if they've never owned a home or land before.

**Key Responsibilities:**

- **Paying Property Taxes on time**
- **Maintaining Homeowners Insurance**
- **Keeping the Property in Good Repair**
- **Handling Utilities, HOA Fees, and Mortgage (if any)**

**Tip:** Include a "Heir Responsibility Letter" with your estate plan outlining these key tasks and deadlines.

# 2. DISCUSS THE CAPITAL GAINS TAX RULES FOR INHERITED PROPERTY

Many heirs rush to sell inherited property, without realizing it could cost them tens of thousands in capital gains taxes if done incorrectly.

**Key Considerations:**

- Inherited property receives a **step-up in basis** at death.
- If they sell the home immediately or within a reasonable time, **little to no capital gains tax** is due.
- But if they **hold the property and it continues to appreciate**, they may owe capital gains tax on the new growth.

**Best Practice:** Consult a CPA before selling any inherited property to avoid surprise tax bills.

# 3. CONSIDER KEEPING THE PROPERTY IN THE FAMILY

Instead of selling, heirs can choose to:

- **Live in the home**
- **Rent it for income**
- **Hold it as a long-term investment**
- **Pass it on to the next generation**

If the property is sentimental (e.g., land, family home, farm), make sure your estate plan:

- **Specifies intent** to keep it
- **Name a family steward or manager**
- Includes an **LLC or trust structure** to manage co-ownership

# 4. USE A FAMILY TRUST OR LLC TO MANAGE LONG-TERM OWNERSHIP

When multiple heirs inherit one property, disagreements or complications often arise. Without structure, it becomes difficult to maintain or make joint decisions.

**Benefits of a Trust or LLC:**

- Appoint a trustee or manager to oversee decisions
- Clarify usage rights and responsibilities
- Protect property from an individual heir's creditors, lawsuits, or divorces
- Define clear rules for selling, renting, or passing it on

**Tip:** Create a Family Property Operating Agreement to prevent future conflict.

# 5. ENCOURAGE HEIRS TO DO THEIR OWN ESTATE PLANNING

Generational wealth only lasts if each generation commits to preserving it.

Encourage your heirs to:

- Create their own **will or trust**
- Add **Transfer on Death** deeds (if legal in their state)
- Stay current on **insurance and taxes**
- Use **financial professionals** to make wise decisions

Don't just pass down the property, pass down the knowledge.

# KEY QUESTIONS TO DISCUSS WITH HEIRS

1. Do you understand the property tax schedule for this home or land?
2. Are you aware of your insurance responsibilities?
3. What's your long-term plan for the property?
4. Would you benefit from renting, selling, or co-owning?
5. Have you spoken with a financial advisor or estate planning attorney?

 

# LEGACY PRESERVATION TIP:

Write a letter to your heirs, sharing:

- Why this property matters to you
- What you hope they'll do with it
- What support systems are in place (trusts, insurance, advisors)
- Your prayer, blessing, or vision for their future

This personal touch can anchor your legacy emotionally, not just legally.

# FINAL WORD:

Passing down property is a victory. But ensuring your family keeps it, grows it, and passes it on again, that's legacy.

**"A good man leaves an inheritance to his children's children." – Proverbs 13:22**

You've taken the steps to build a legacy. Now empower your family to protect and preserve it.

# BONUS: HOW TO PROTECT INHERITED PROPERTY FROM BECOMING A MARITAL ASSET

## 1. LEAVE PROPERTY IN A TRUST

Using a **Revocable Living Trust or Irrevocable Trust** to pass down property offers the best protection.

**How It Works:**

- You place the property in a trust and name your heir as the beneficiary (not the direct owner).
- The trust can include **language that explicitly keeps the inheritance separate** from marital assets.
- In the event of divorce, the property remains owned by the trust, not the individual, so it cannot be divided.

**Pro Tip:** Consider an *Irrevocable Trust* if you're serious about permanently protecting the asset (e.g., from lawsuits, creditors, or future divorces).

 

# 2. INCLUDE BLOODLINE PROTECTION CLAUSES IN YOUR TRUST OR WILL

When drafting estate planning documents, include clauses that:

- Define that only **biological descendants** (children, grandchildren) may inherit or benefit from the property.
- Prohibit selling or transferring the property to spouses or in-laws.
- Require property to remain **within the family line** through each generation.

This is sometimes called a "**Family Legacy Clause**" or "**Bloodline Trust**" provision.

# 3. AVOID PUTTING THE PROPERTY INTO JOINT OWNERSHIP AFTER INHERITANCE

If the heir:

- Adds their spouse's name to the deed, or
- Uses marital funds for upkeep or renovation,

the inherited property may become **commingled**, losing its protection as separate property.

**Solution:** Instruct heirs to keep inherited property in their name only and avoid using joint accounts to pay for it.

 

# 4. HAVE THE HEIR SIGN A PRENUPTIAL OR POSTNUPTIAL AGREEMENT

If the heir is married or planning to marry:

- A **prenup** or **postnup** can clarify that the inherited property is separate and **not subject to division** in divorce.
- It should also address appreciation in value and rental income, which may otherwise become marital property.

This agreement should be drafted by an attorney and signed willingly by both spouses.

# 5. TITLE PROPERTY IN AN LLC OWNED BY A TRUST

For rental properties, family farmland, or shared heir property:

- Title the property in an LLC (Limited Liability Company)
- The LLC is then owned by the trust

This creates an additional legal barrier, keeps control centralized, and adds protection from lawsuits, divorces, and creditors.

**Bonus:** LLCs can include operating agreements with ownership restrictions (e.g., no transfers to non-family members).

# EXAMPLE SCENARIO

**Without Protection:**
You leave your home to your daughter outright. She adds her husband to the deed, and they renovate it together. Years later, they divorce, and he's legally entitled to part of the home's value.

**With Protection:**
You leave the home in a trust for your daughter. The trust states that she can live in it, rent it, or pass it to her children, but not transfer it to a spouse. Her husband has no legal claim to the home, even in divorce.

This agreement should be drafted by an attorney and signed willingly by both spouses.

# FINAL WARNING:

Even if property is inherited separately, it can still be lost in divorce if the heir doesn't:

- Keep it titled in their name or trust
- Avoid commingling marital funds
- Protect the asset with legal agreements or trust structures

# DISCLAIMER

This content is for educational and informational purposes only and is not intended as legal, tax, or financial advice.

While I am a Financial Coach and Educator, I am not an attorney, CPA, or licensed tax advisor.

Before making any decisions related to estate planning, real estate transfers, or tax strategies, please consult with a qualified estate attorney, tax professional, or real estate expert in your jurisdiction.

Laws vary by state and individual circumstances. Use of this material does not create a client relationship or guarantee specific results.

Journey to Generational Wealth® is committed to empowering individuals through education; however, final decisions should always be made in consultation with licensed professionals.

# DON'T FORGET YOUR TOOLKIT!

Before you dive in, make sure you have the "Keep It In The Family" Property Transfer Toolkit by your side. This companion resource includes **fillable worksheets, checklists, and planning templates** to help you **take action** and **protect your legacy with clarity and confidence.**

You're not just here to learn - you're here to build.

Visit: www.journeytogenerationalwealth.com/product-page/propertytransfertoolkit

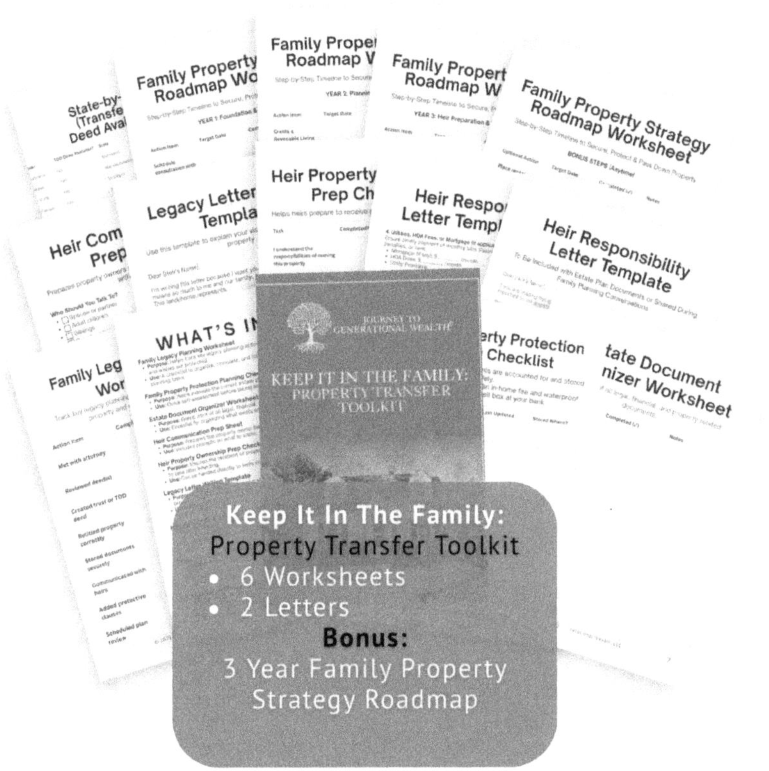


 

# KEEP LEARNING, KEEP GROWING

## Explore More From Journey to Generational Wealth®

Your financial journey doesn't stop here. Continue building your knowledge, protecting your legacy, and positioning your family for generational success with these powerful resources. Each eBook is designed to educate and empower, and most come with a companion toolkit to help you take real action.

### The Smart Saver's Guide to High-Yield Savings Accounts (HYSA)

Learn how to grow your savings faster with high-yield accounts and make your money work harder for you.

**Get the Companion: Smart Saver's Toolkit**

### Maximize Your Money with a Money Market Account

Learn how to make the most of your money by using a Money Market Account to earn more interest while keeping your money accessible.

### The Financial Foolery Detox

Detox from money myths, reset your mindset, and finally get clear on your financial goals.

### Keep It In The Family: Passing Down Property Without Probate

Learn how to grow your savings faster with high-yield accounts and make your money work harder for you.

**Get the Companion: Property Transfer Toolkit**

### Keep It In The Family: Why Life Insurance Is a Must for Building Black Wealth

Learn how to grow your savings faster with high-yield accounts and make your money work harder for you.

**Get the Companion: Life Insurance Readiness Toolkit**

### Legacy Matters: The Legacy Blueprint

A step-by-step guide to protecting what you've built and passing it on with purpose.

**Get the Companion: Legacy Planning Toolkit**

Shop all eBooks:
www.journeytogenerationalwealth.com/ebooks-toolkits

# REFERENCES

American Bar Association. (n.d.). Probate FAQ. https://www.americanbar.org/groups/real_property_trust_estate/resources/estate_planning/probate_faq/

American College of Trust and Estate Counsel. (n.d.). Why do I need a trust? https://www.actec.org/estate-planning/why-do-i-need-a-trust/

CNBC Select. (2023, July 17). How to avoid taxes on inherited property. https://www.cnbc.com/select/how-to-avoid-tax-on-inherited-property/

Consumer Financial Protection Bureau. (n.d.). Managing someone else's money. https://www.consumerfinance.gov/consumer-tools/managing-someone-elses-money/

Fidelity Investments. (n.d.). Step-up in basis: What it is and why it matters. https://www.fidelity.com/learning-center/personal-finance/tax-basics/step-up-in-basis

Forbes Advisor. (2023, August 2). Inherited property in divorce. https://www.forbes.com/advisor/legal/divorce/inherited-property-in-divorce/

Internal Revenue Service. (n.d.-a). Estate and gift taxes. https://www.irs.gov/businesses/small-businesses-self-employed/estate-and-gift-taxes

 

# REFERENCES

Internal Revenue Service. (n.d.-b). Publication 559: Survivors, executors, and administrators. https://www.irs.gov/forms-pubs/about-publication-559

Internal Revenue Service. (n.d.-c). Topic no. 409 capital gains and losses. https://www.irs.gov/taxtopics/tc409

Investopedia. (2023, March 21). Marital property: Definition, what's included, and laws. https://www.investopedia.com/terms/m/maritalproperty.asp

LegalZoom. (2022, November 15). How much does probate cost? https://www.legalzoom.com/articles/how-much-does-probate-cost

National Association of Estate Planners & Councils. (n.d.). About estate planning. https://www.naepc.org/

National Conference of State Legislatures. (2023, February). Property taxation. https://www.ncsl.org/research/fiscal-policy/property-taxation.aspx

National Notary Association. (2022, May 18). Notarizing estate planning documents. https://www.nationalnotary.org/knowledge-center/about-notaries/notary-basics/notarizing-estate-planning-documents

 

# REFERENCES

NerdWallet. (2023, March 10). What to do after inheriting a house. https://www.nerdwallet.com/article/mortgages/what-to-do-inheriting-house

Nolo. (n.d.-a). How to avoid probate. https://www.nolo.com/legal-encyclopedia/avoiding-probate

Nolo. (n.d.-b). Which states allow transfer on death deeds? https://www.nolo.com/legal-encyclopedia/which-states-allow-transfer-on-death-deeds.html

Nolo. (n.d.-c). Using trusts to shield assets from creditors. https://www.nolo.com/legal-encyclopedia/trusts-shielding-assets-from-creditors

Tax Foundation. (2024, January 2). State inheritance and estate tax map. https://taxfoundation.org/data/all/state/state-estate-tax-inheritance-tax-2024/

U.S. Courts. (n.d.). Probate matters. https://www.uscourts.gov/services-forms/probate-matters

U.S. Department of Housing and Urban Development. (n.d.). Homeownership resources. https://www.hud.gov/topics/homeownership

Loeb & Loeb LLP. (2025, July 9). The One Big Beautiful Bill Act: Breaking down key changes in the new tax legislation. https://www.loeb.com/en/insights/publications/2025/07/the-one-big-beautiful-bill-act-breaking-down-key-changes-in-the-new-tax-legislation

Kiplinger. (2025, July 8). Estate tax exemption permanently raised: What it means for families. https://www.kiplinger.com/taxes/whats-the-new-estate-tax-exemption

 

# ABOUT THE AUTHOR

Laura Sanders, MBA, is a passionate Financial Educator, Author, Speaker, and the visionary Founder of Journey to Generational Wealth® and Creations Publishing. With a deep commitment to financial literacy and legacy building, Laura empowers women of color and families to break generational cycles of financial instability and create lasting wealth.

As a financial coach and licensed life insurance agent, Laura has dedicated her life to equipping others with the knowledge and tools necessary to manage their finances wisely, protect their assets, and pass down generational wealth. She brings a powerful blend of lived experience, professional expertise, and community care to every book, workbook, and program she creates.

Through her children's books, journals, toolkits, and educational resources, Laura makes complex financial topics accessible and practical for all ages. Whether she's teaching a child how to save or guiding a family through money management, her goal remains the same: to help others build a future rooted in stability, security, and legacy.

When she's not coaching, writing or teaching, Laura enjoys creating intentional moments with her child and inspiring others to believe that financial freedom is possible, no matter where you're starting from.

Learn more and explore her resources at www.journeytogenerationalwealth.com

JOURNEY TO
GENERATIONAL WEALTH®

# STILL HAVE QUESTIONS?

**Email Your Questions to:**

info@journeytogenerationalwealth.com

# NEED FURTHER ASSISTANCE WITH YOUR FINANCES?

**Schedule a Financial Clarity Session:**

https://www.journeytogenerationalwealth.com/financial-clarity-session

www.ingramcontent.com/pod-product-compliance
Lightning Source LLC
LaVergne TN
LVHW022029200926
848481LV00007B/2615